THE UNCENSORED BOY'S OWN

THE UNCENSORED
BOY'S OWN

By
Dick Beresford

Macdonald

With thanks to the illustrators of boys' stories
in the period 1925–35

A MACDONALD BOOK

First published in Great Britain in 1990
by Macdonald & Co (Publishers) Ltd
London & Sydney

Conceived, edited and designed by Russell Ash and Bernard Higton
© 1990 Russell Ash and Bernard Higton

Reproduced, printed and bound in Great Britain by
Richard Clay Ltd, Bungay, Suffolk

British Library Cataloguing in Publication Data
Beresford, Dick
The uncensored Boy's own.
1. humorous cartoons
I. Title
741.5942

ISBN 0 356 19508 2

Macdonald & Co (Publishers) Ltd
Orbit House
1 New Fetter Lane
London EC4A 1AR

A member of Maxwell Macmillan Pergamon Publishing Corporation

CONTENTS

LIFE AT ST. FRED'S

I started at St Wilfrid's ("St Fred's", we called it) and was
immediately introduced to the school's bizarre
initiation ritual. All the new boys were kitted out with
sun-ray goggles and led into Matron's bedroom where we were
smeared with tartar sauce. It was never explained why.

The other school customs were quite strange too: take the
annual "Toppers v Boaters" match that was fought on
Fred's Bottom, a part of the playing fields. Any boy who
managed permanently to maim another scored a
point for his House.

The annual Inter-school Mincing Competition was always popular among a certain type of boy, and for weeks beforehand they could be seen hard at work practising for the hard-fought contest.

Then there was "Hide an Onion up the Chimney Day", held
on the third Wednesday after Septuagesima.

The Saturday night "hop" to which the local Italian waiters were
traditionally invited was, I think, unique to St Fred's.

The quality of tuition was frankly pretty appalling.
"It's a real stumper!" was the general reaction when we were asked
"What is the capital of France?"

I can't say St Fred's was exactly brilliant at
sports, and we resorted to various ploys to give us the
edge over our opponents: disposing of the ref
before the game started was one.

On another occasion, when we were being slightly trounced
in a rugby match against St Wilgefortis Third XV (165 nil, if I
remember correctly), young Fanshaw cunningly arranged
to have 25 truck loads of horse manure delivered to the pitch,
and the game was thankfully called off.

The school polo team's away match with the Argentinians
turned rather ugly.

Extra-curricular activities were encouraged and,
although I nearly left my entry behind, I managed to win
the school taxidermy prize (the Jemima Pogworthy Prize for
Dog-Mounting, to give it its correct title).

There were many mysterious things about St Fred's. It always puzzled me that all the boys in Form 5A were Japanese, and why *did* Ripley have a detailed street map of Bognor tattooed on his chest?

And had Tichborne *really* strained his right arm
writing his entry for the school Poetry Prize, or was there
some more sinister explanation?

Some of the boys had singular talents.
Larwood was famed throughout
the school for his immensely powerful
technique of breaking wind.
We were astonished by the sheer
volume, and he became
something of a hero among the
younger boys.

Sadly, while he was asking
me about his trigonometry prep,
he stood too close to the fire
and when he let rip
he spontaneously combusted.

Angus McPratt, our Head of House, was possibly
the worst bagpipe player who ever lived. Back home, the only
living creatures he could persuade to listen to his ghastly
dirges were the famous tone-deaf seals of Mull.

Jesmond had a morbid fear of cats, so for a jape we
went to the local herbalist and bought a packet of dried *Valeriana
officinalis*, a herb that cats love, and smeared it all over
him. After he'd been attacked by half a dozen crazed moggies,
he was removed to the sanatorium a gibbering wreck.

Simpson, the boy soprano, was a dashed rum cove. Sometimes he would wake up in the middle of the night and sing an aria from *Die Fledermaus*.

And I'll never forget Harbottle, who was always trying to unscrew his fag's head.

There were some embarrassing moments – like when Francis
was hauled before the beak to explain why he had thrown up in
the Major's hat. Just as he was denying it, in marched the
Major with the evidence in his hand.

Then there was the time Warrington Minor
swallowed a ferret.

I can't deny that bullying was rife
at St Fred's. Arm-twisting the juniors was
a particular favourite.

Occasionally, some of the older boys would take a
horsewhip to Jarvis, the Head's senile old butler.

Sometimes the Head Boy would have Jarvis
thrown out of the library window.

Even at St Fred's it was thought unusual to be chauffeured to class, but Oxley's father, Horatio Oxley (the cog-wheel magnate), made sure his son wanted for nothing.

He was excessively spoilt and frankly rather violent. We always thought that calling his Indian houseboy into the dorm in the middle of the night so he could give him a good thrashing was going a bit far.

As the years passed, Oxley became increasingly aggressive.
He took to wearing a woolly hat, and woebetide anyone
who dared comment on it.

He went on through life punching everyone in sight . . .

. . . and after being expelled from St Fred's went
to work in the design department of his
father's cog-wheel factory. There he apparently
beat a fellow worker to death for touching
his set-square and was hanged for murder – only
the 27th convicted murderer in St Fred's
glorious 80-year history.

OLD MASTERS

Some of the masters at St Fred's were a bit queer. There was Hogson, for instance, who charged us half-a-crown a lesson.

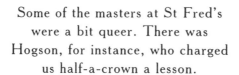

And why did Signor Fonzini, the music master, always conduct the school orchestra through the window and make us wear dressing gowns and smoke pipes? This was one of the many questions to which I never received a satisfactory answer.

Miss Roberts' impromptu demonstrations of the Mauritian
national dance invariably emptied the class.

Once the Head dragged me out into the snow
and, kneeling down, declared, "There! Do you see them?
The tracks of the Giant Peruvian Wildebeest!"
He was barking mad.

Mr Pargeter, the Religious Instruction teacher,
had some unusual ideas. One night, donning white tie and
tails, he invited a few boys into a darkened room
where, he claimed, we could witness the ethereal power
of the Mystic Crystal Pyramid of Loomis.

Our Housemaster Mr Clemens bore an uncanny resemblance
to Mark Twain, and there were those who believed
he was a distant cousin. This was reinforced when he showed us
a film of *Tom Sawyer* – at least, that's what he said it was,
but it was an unusual version in which none of the boys wore clothes.
Mr Clemens explained it was to emphasise the
naturalness of the story.

I once spotted him sneaking furtively out of the school in
full evening dress. I followed him into the village
and saw him going into the Pink Pussycat nightclub, where he
mingled with the *demi-monde* of rural Bedfordshire.

It was there he met Monsieur Lautrec, a local artist
who he persuaded to paint a portrait of young
Carraway as Tom Sawyer (as a result of which
Carraway sadly caught pneumonia).

Any boy who Mr Clemens took a dislike to might be
blindfolded and pushed over a bucket, or he would be
handed a lighted firework.

Mr Clemens was, frankly, power-mad. He never
quite understood that he didn't have the right to sentence
a Third-Former to death.

His behaviour grew more and more peculiar until
one night, returning to school rather the worse for wear, he
ran amok in the dorm and was finally pensioned off.

The twin history masters, Mr Fortescue and
Mr Fortescue, were also rather strange. I heard that they
belonged to an exclusive gentlemen-only rumba club,
from which they often had to be collected by cab in a
state of advanced intoxication.

One night, Carstairs and I found one of the Mr
Fortescues (I was never sure which) bound and gagged.
When we undid him, he spluttered something about
how he'd been doing some macramé and had "got into a
bit of a tangle", but we didn't really believe him.

Another night I heard a strange noise coming from
the school cellar. When I went down to investigate, there were
both Mr Fortescues chained up, as happy as sandboys.
"We'd invite you to join us," smirked one of them, "but I'm afraid
we've only got two neck rings."
Needless to say, I made an excuse and left.

Of course, I was an innocent. I should have suspected
something when they invited me to be guest of honour at a
meeting of the Edward II Society. Fortuitously,
Carstairs, the good egg, had hidden in the wardrobe
and leapt out in the nick of time.
The Head, I recall, paid me a tidy
sum to keep mum about the
whole sorry incident.

Advice for Boys

We were always warned not to speak to strange men.
If it was rumoured that there was a boy-spotter in the
vicinity, we were confined to school.

When I was quite young I was taking a stroll in the
woods when a stranger emerged from the trees. Out of his
jodphurs he whipped an object the like of which I
had never seen before, which he brandished before my
astonished eyes. Then he muttered something about the
batteries being flat, and went off in a filthy bate.

When you get a lot of boys living together it's
inevitable that a certain amount of beastliness occurs,
and St Fred's was no exception. This was perhaps
encouraged to some extent by the unusual rule that boys
should economise on laundry by sharing a bed.

The staff, it would be true to say, took an enlightened
attitude to these boyish friendships, masters even
offering advice on suitable pairings. Mr Crisp, the art
teacher, had a particular penchant for "fixing boys up"
with young gardeners, but the time he
sent a ship's stoker to Cleaver's study
was not a howling success.

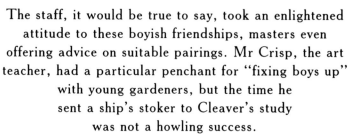

The relationship of Hinckley and Witherspoon, I think,
encapsulated the frequently charming nature of these
friendships. They could often be seen just sitting
quietly together down at the pavilion discussing what a
horrid, rough game cricket was.

Things got a bit out of hand when they tried to elope.

They bickered on the train when a boy from
a state school insisted on puffing a pipe full of shag
in their compartment.

They were eventually stopped by
private detectives when Hinckley, disguised
as a travelling salesman, stepped off
the train at Gretna Green.

I'd be the first to admit it took a while
to find out about, you know,
persons of the opposite gender and all
that. I think it was Hamilton who first
aroused my interest.
"Never mind about making model
aircraft," he blurted. "I've just
found out about GIRLS!"

So much of what he told me sounded unbelievable,
and he wasn't too sure himself about some
of the finer points, that we decided to sneak into
the school library and look up everything we
could on the subject.

The inadequacy of the library on such matters was
immediately apparent, but Matron tried to help out by
showing us some interesting photographs.

We took one of the photos away with us and examined it in
detail, but we were still completely baffled.

Then one day during the holidays I was browsing in
a secondhand bookshop when I chanced upon a volume called
Psycopathia Sexualis by a man called Krafft-Ebing.
I had to translate it from Latin, but it told me more than I ever
thought possible about certain practices, and travelling back
to school I told the other chaps about them. At first
they didn't believe a word, especially all that stuff about the
gerbils and the butter.

We got a bit confused trying out some of the ideas.

I admit I got off on the wrong foot and
started taking an interest in very young girls,
which rather shocked the other chaps

Hanging "art studies" of Matron was frowned on.

One summer I met Brenda, the Head Girl
at our sister school, St Winifred's.

It was a rather progressive school at which bullfighting
was a compulsory subject

Unlike the other girls, Brenda had no time for schoolgirl
crushes, and when a prefect, Angela Paraguay
I think her name was, made what she described as "an
improper advance", she picked up a grand piano
and threw it at her.

She was, however, absolutely hopeless at cricket,
so I soon lost interest.

The caretaker Blenkinsop's lad
would always run errands in the village,
picking up the odd packet
of this and that.

Sometimes Scott would get hold of a giant economy pack,
which he'd generously pass round. Naturally, chewing gum was
strictly forbidden, so we had to be jolly careful.

BE PREPARED!

I had been in the Wolf Cubs, which was ripping fun.
Akela really threw herself into the spirit of our camps.

At St Fred's, I joined the 121st Bedfordshire Boy Scout Troop.
Playing "chicken" with express trains was one of our
favourite games – until the fateful day that Carraway didn't quite
make it. His mangled body was identified by his woggle.

The Troop was full of surprises. There was Dregthorpe,
for instance, who refused to wear the uniform, and could not be
parted from his cuddly bunny, and McGoolie, whose
legs were completely invisible.

Harcourt was obsessed with the occult. He believed anyone
who wasn't a Boy Scout must be a vampire.

He thought running into ghostly highwayman was clever.
What a bore!

Pilchard got into a lot of trouble with the local farmers
when he suffocated their sheep.

And there was the time his bob-a-job went wrong when he
tried to polish Lord Elsey's Bentley with a Brillo pad.

Our camps were packed with incident, like the time we saw
a Thuggee assassin skulking outside our tents.

We later discovered that he had kidnapped
the Scout Master.

Then there was the occasion when a ruffian came to camp
and offered to barter a Scout for a basket of eggs.

He later raised his offer to a bull, and this time
was accompanied by a mysterious German wearing a pyjama
jacket and wellingtons.

Soon afterwards, two bullies dragged me to the house where
the German fellow lived. "*Schweinhund!*" he ejaculated.
"I specifically ordered *two* Boy Scouts!" While he ranted,
I managed to wriggle free and escape.

The kraut leaped onto his horse and chased me into
the woods, but the horse stumbled and he fell off. The Scout
Master found him lying there, moaning. "You two boys,
come here!" he demanded. "Remember what I taught you about
the kiss of life?" The German soon came round and
had a funny sort of smile on his face.

With One Leap...

Few of the school trips were unrivalled successes – after all,
you don't expect to be captured by Incas in Surbiton.
Fortuntely, just as I was about to be sacrificed to one of
their heathen gods, there was a freak earthquake (again, not
something that happens every day in Surrey), and I managed
to break free as my captors were swallowed up.

On another occasion I just escaped being sacrificed to the
Blind Buddha of Penge and attacked by the Mad Minotaur
of Mitcham, had a near miss with the Deadly Druids of
Dagenham and shot the Grinning Gorilla of Godalming, and
all before prep – but that's another story.

The initiative test trip to Spain was even more eventful.
We were sent off without luggage, given just sixpence each and
told to expect the unexpected. We weren't disappointed.
We each chose a different means of getting there, plucky
little Farnsworth setting off on his trusty bike.

Grimshaw and Lucas opted for a more laborious method.
"If I'd known it would be like this", spluttered Grimshaw,
"I'd never have bought shares in Eurotunnel."

For those who took the supposedly easy route there was
a really rough Channel crossing.

Show-off Doggett thought he'd make headlines for himself by
surfing across, on his back with a smelly tramp lashed on
top of him. They were both drowned, of course.

Burgwallis had a slight altercation with the Customs.

Strang and Catchpole, who had absolutely no
sense of direction at all, found themselves shinning up the
north face of the Eiger.

Later they fetched up in Matebeleland.

Richardson attempted a somewhat reckless air crossing.

Meanwhile Murchison and I walked down to Dover, grabbed
a handy amphibious vehicle and simply drove across.

We swiped a car and headed south, with the police in hot pursuit.
Unfortunately Murchison was a really terrible driver.

Eventually he drove our Bugatti straight into the side
of a building which, as luck would have it, turned out to be
a Spanish police station!

We were caught and
when they mocked Murchison's
favourite piece of string . . .

. . . . he went berserk.

In the confusion I got away, but Murchison was sentenced
to 30 years' hard labour as prisoner 19, though – typical jammy
Murchison this – he was later promoted to 797.

The Big Match

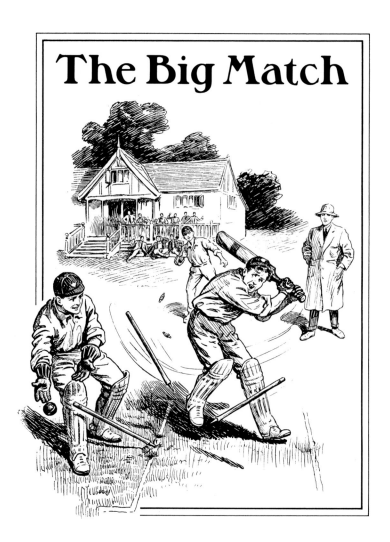

It was the day of the Big Match against St Wilgefortis.
They fielded a team of ringers (nine professionals and two
games masters). We had words with them before the match
started and suggested that pipe-smoking players with
moustaches were not exactly what one expected in a
supposedly Fifth-Form team, but they wouldn't have any of
it and opened with a couple of demons who scored a corking
794 for 0 declared before lunch.

Peg-leg Wilkins was perhaps an unusual choice for our
opening bat, and partnered by "Dozy" Dinsdale, who never
knew which end of the pitch he was supposed to be
standing, the result was disastrous. Wilkins managed to clip
the first ball to leg (his real leg, that is), but when he
attempted to run screwed himself into the ground. He was
out next ball – though "Stump Before Wicket" was a new
one on most of us.

St Wilgefortis' dirty tricks department
pulled out all the stops. A fiendish bouncer got
Esdaile out (for keeps, so it turned out).
Our Captain remonstrated with theirs, but he just told him
that the odd death was something every team had to
face up to and not to be such a bunch of cissies.

Then – and this really was a poor
show – they sent a telegram to Carruthers
just as he was going into bat,
telling him his pet shrew had died.
He was so unnerved that he
was out first ball.

With the score standing at 0 for 9, I went into bat.
I can tell you, I felt rather nervous. I skied the first one over
the pavilion and by tea had notched up 795. Apart
from winning the Jemima Pogworthy Prize for Dog-Mounting,
this was perhaps the best day of the best years of my
life at St Fred's.